An A
With Banners

A book on banners for the Church of Christ

by Priscilla Nunnerley

This book is dedicated to many friends in the fellowship of The King's Church, Amersham, Buckinghamshire, and especially to those who have shared in banner-making.

First published in 1982
1st reprint 1984
2nd reprint 1986
3rd reprint 1988

ISBN 0 9509307 0 9

All photographs and drawings are, unless otherwise stated, of banners made in Amersham. Those on pages 62 and 63 were made in Scotland. We are grateful for the kind permission of St Michael-le-Belfrey, York, to print photographs and to include a chapter on their banners.

Production and printing in England by
Nuprint Limited, 30b Station Road, Harpenden, Herts AL5 4SE

Contents

The following measurements of some of the banners in the colour section may be helpful:

Photographs 1, 11, 12 and 13: 7 ft–8 ft (213 cm–244 cm)

Photograph 2: 57 in × 30 in (145 cm × 76 cm)

Photograph 3: 54 in × 24 in (137 cm × 61 cm)

Photograph 6: 47 in sq (120 cm sq)

Photograph 7: 35 in × 59 in (89 cm × 150 cm)

Photograph 9: 45 in × 53 in (115 cm × 135 cm)

Introduction

After four years of banner-making I felt that God wanted me to share what was happening in our group. People were intrigued by the simplicity of the banners they saw in our church and homes and wanted to know more. Several groups sprung from ours.

As the Fisherfolk were our original inspiration I decided to ask if I might visit them to discuss the subject. Crossing on New Year's Day 1978 to the Isle of Cumbrae I spent a Sunday with them and was encouraged to go ahead with the project. They themselves were occupied with music but suggested I visit the group at St Michael-le-Belfrey, York.

The aims of this book are to show how banners can be inspired by the Holy Spirit and how the making of them is a spiritual ministry that does not necessarily involve artistic skills or sewing abilities. It is an immense privilege to seek for just the right word from the heart of the Lord that will then speak to His people.

I had recently left junior teaching and was working for the social services when I wrote the main part of this book. Both jobs helped me to communicate in a clear and straightforward way, aiming to meet needs, rather than give unnecessary information. Most important of all I had learnt that, when working in a group situation, it is more important to encourage others to make and create than to dominate and be successful oneself.

If you are to lead a little group to make banners you need some enthusiasm and a vision of what is needed. You do not have to be a strong leader but can see yourself as co-ordinator, catalyst and, most of all, encourager.

Although it is good to have fresh inspiration for each banner it is impossible to be entirely original and so you are welcome to use some of our ideas and designs in creating your own.

Unless stated our banners are fairly small, measuring from 18 in × 2 ft (45 cm × 60 cm) to 2 ft × 3 ft (60 cm × 92 cm).

Banners today

The art of banner-making is returning. Banners in churches have been limited to elaborate traditional designs of great beauty and detail. Now the simplicity of the art is being revived as Christians are seeking to express the fullness of life in Jesus that the Holy Spirit is bringing to the church world-wide. Christians are making banners to praise the Lord, to celebrate His love and proclaim His salvation.

Banner-making is being restored, not as a ladies' sewing circle but as a spiritual ministry. If you look down an avenue of trees you see them appear to merge on the horizon and banners, like the avenue, can focus our attention but on God.

Ideas for such banners come through prayer and meditation and out of everyday life. They are an expression of what is happening now and a fresh interpretation of the Word of God for a certain church, group or individual. They communicate life because they grow out of fellowship with the Lord.

As a flag blows in the wind so movement is in the message and beauty of these banners. As a battle standard led the people on so these banners direct people forward to a God who is going ahead of His people. Because they can be easily made, hung and removed they bring a sense of the immediacy of the living Word of God.

Banners are not an end in themselves but a natural outcome of our life in God, leading us on into a deeper knowledge of the Lord and His will. They are just one of the joyous art-forms that the Spirit has brought back in the last days to herald the Return of the King.

One day, with all preparation over, Jesus will reign as King of Kings and Lord of Lords. Meanwhile, I believe our Creator would wish His children to celebrate and express His love as part of our inheritance, to glorify His Name and exalt His Son.

The risen Christ breaks out of the grave with power and victory reassuring His followers that He is Lord.

IT IS I MYSELF

Banners in warfare

by Evelyn Lucas and Priscilla Nunnerley

Why are banners mentioned in the Bible?

In the Old Testament banners were a rallying point in battle to unify those fighting by giving them a visible reminder of their identity. Banners were their inspiration and encouragement and the role of the standard bearer was a vital one. If the banner was still flying it meant the bearer, in the thick of battle, was still fighting. Moses declares 'The Lord is my Banner' Exodus 17:15. Isaiah writes of the Spirit of the Lord lifting up a standard against the enemy when he comes in like a flood.

Why banners in history?

Banners continued on through history, being used at the Crusades and many other battles including the American Civil War. They are the origin of what we know as flags of different countries. There are regimental colours in places like Westminster Abbey. Banners were also widely used in craft guilds and are still used in Trade Union marches. All have a place of pride in the memories of men who marched beneath them.

Why did the old hymn-writers use the banner image in so many of their hymns?

Because they were aware that they were in a great cosmic struggle with God against unseen powers of wickedness in high places

> 'Stand up, stand up for Jesus, ye soldiers of the cross
> Lift high His royal banner, it must not suffer loss.'

This is the hymn of a people who recognized they were under battle orders from the Captain of the hosts of heaven.

In recent years Christians have compromised with vital issues and so the church has lost much of its fighting spirit. Where are the banners today? Still to be seen in society at union protest marches and in processions for other causes. Why? Because these people are still fighting their battles.

How can we use banners today?

In our fight against the principalities and powers of darkness we may soon be able to take today's banners out from the church into the market place, to be carried in processions, held aloft at rallies and used on television. Imagine the impact of a procession with a hundred flags waving, each one different but all for the cause of Christ. The impact could be as strong and powerful as a two-edged sword. We do not have to make costly or elaborate banners; they should be simple enough for children to help. Let us get them made so that we can hold them high to the glory of God.

Beauty among the people of God

Beauty is coming back into many areas of worship. The Psalmist talks of longing to dwell in the House of the Lord, to behold His beauty. Although external beauty is not an essential requirement for worship it can convey a little glimmer of the beauty of our Lord. Much thought and expense is often given to furnishing a living room and making it attractive, so should we not give care and attention to the place where we meet for worship?

Beauty is exciting and can quicken the senses and open the spirit to joy. To some extent what we see determines what we become. The divine plan is for us to be 'a crown of beauty in the hand of the Lord'. His gift of beauty has been stored away for too long. Let's get it out and enjoy it! Let's exult in the wonder and riches of our God and seek to express them in visible and tangible ways. Music, flowers, furnishings, paintings, sculptures, dance and banners can contribute to seeing 'the King in his beauty'.

A gift given back to the giver

Any Christian can take part in making banners because the making of them is primarily a spiritual ministry and therefore artistic ability is not a necessary requirement. This cannot be too heavily emphasised. Those who are new to the idea and join a small group can start by cutting out letters and sewing hems and so contribute to a bigger project. A simple banner can be made by someone working independently.

Natural talents offered to the Lord are touched and then transformed to become a spiritual gift to glorify God and build up the body of Christ with unlimited opportunity to grow and develop. For most this will not be banner-making. It may be gardening or car maintenance, music or dancing, woodwork or cookery.

Margery hates sewing and is not naturally artistic but has a banner as a wall-hanging in her home. Once she shared with others how it came to be made. She said: 'I felt we should have a banner in our home so that as people come in they know the Lord is here. Bruce liked the idea. I phoned a friend and arranged a meeting to discuss it. I sat down on the settee and wondered what to do. The words came into my mind:

> "You shall love the Lord your God
> with all your heart, with all your soul
> and with all your strength"

These words tell that our love for Him must come first.

I went to the meeting thrilled that Lord had given me this banner. It hardly cost anything to make. The background material is curtain fabric, left over from the living room curtains. The flowers are cut from another fabric. The only thing I bought was the felt. How it's helped me as I've passed it in the hall. It's been a constant reminder to put God first!'

Margery stayed with the group making banners for the

Church and other folks for nearly two years. By her very presence she made the most important contribution, that of herself. With encouragement and help she was drawn into cutting letters and stitching, choosing, shopping and glueing. We shared our lives and got to know each other and that was, perhaps, more important than the banners we made.

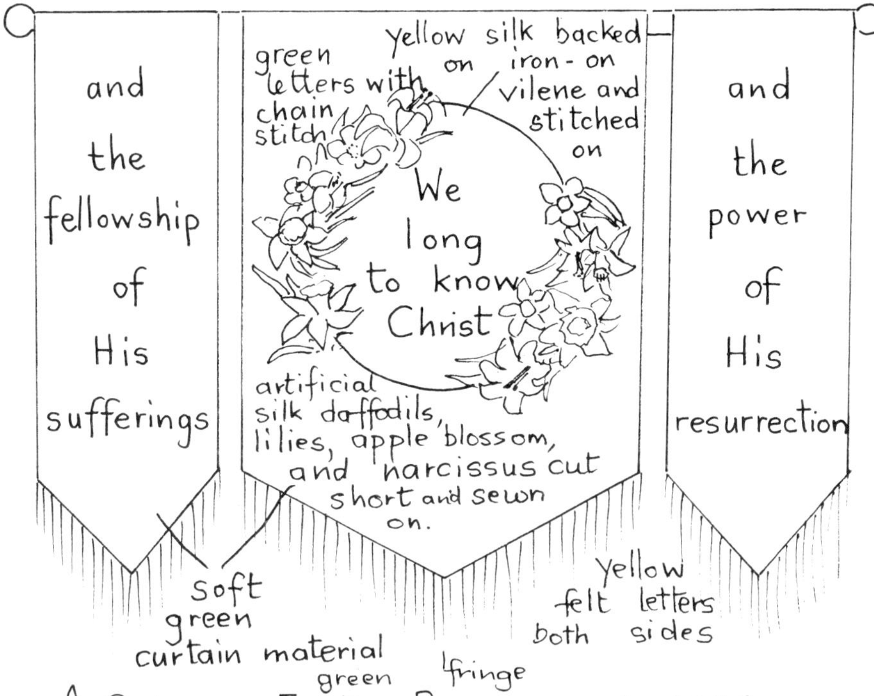

A Spring or Easter Banner made 1982.

The Word on banners

A most important part of banners, we believe, is the Word of God. The aim of our banners is to lift the Word before the people so they see it, absorb it, meditate on it, remember and obey it. Words portrayed visually can be retained by the memory much longer than the spoken word.

The psalmist says, 'Thy statutes have been my songs in the house of my pilgrimage'. The Word is our delight, our refreshing, our bread, our strength, our light, our guide and our life. The man who meditates on the law of God continually is called blessed (Psalm 1). He is likened to a tree whose roots go down deep into the water and can still bear green leaves in time of drought. (See colour photograph 9).

The words of the Bible have the power of no other words. I have seen a church banner around some words given in a vision, and although the banner was beautiful and was of help to that particular congregation, it didn't have the universal power of the Word of God.

The words of scripture and the search for God can be echoed in hymns and these too can be used. One banner was made for Whitsun with the words 'Come down, O Love Divine' and they were clear and fitting for that occasion.

Scripture can be used in the following ways on banners:

To proclaim:

Jesus is Lord
God was in Christ
The free gift of God is eternal life in Christ Jesus

To celebrate:

Celebrate the harvest with joy
The two shall become one
He is risen

To strengthen and comfort:

His banner over me is love
God is faithful
Nothing shall separate us from the Love of God
He lives to make intercession

To challenge:

Watch and pray
What does the Lord require of you?
Go into all the world

To command:

Rejoice in the Lord
Watch and pray
Freely you have received; freely give
Love one another
Bear ye one another's burdens

To promise:

I will return
I will pour my Spirit upon you
I will come to you
If we confess our sins, He is faithful and just to forgive us our sins and to cleanse us from all unrighteousness

To command and promise:

Bring the full tithes and I will open the windows of heaven
Ask and you will receive
Seek and you will find
Knock and it shall be opened unto you

Banners without words

The Word is not only verses of Scripture, it is Jesus Himself, the Word made flesh. It is not always appropriate or necessary to communicate through words. As there are times when a loving hug or kiss can meet a deeper need than words so in art there are times and places where Christ Himself is shown clearly and deeply through a drawing, painting, sculpture or collage. The art form itself ministers His life to us. When the Word of God is used with a design it conveys a specific thought whereas a design without words leaves the interpretation open and ministers Jesus to meet widely different aspirations, hopes and needs.

An example of this was a little banner made for the Primary Sunday School. We found the picture in the Scripture Union Guide which prefaces one edition of the Good News Bible.

The drawing shows Jesus holding a toddler while a little girl tugs his robe. Another girl is skipping with joy and a boy is kneeling before Him and looking up into His face. Clare enlarged the drawing and I drew patterns for the figures. Margery chose the background and coloured felts and cut out shapes and letters and appliquéd them on with unobtrusive stitching. The vivid primary colours are ones which young children appreciate and the whole picture shows the warm and affectionate love of Jesus for children. 22 in × 24 in, (56 × 61 cm).

Finding the right word for a banner

Our task is to seek and knock. If we really believe that God sends His Word forth to accomplish a specific goal, we must enquire of Him for each specific assignment. God sends forth His Word to reveal, to remind, to restore. He is able to sustain with a Word him that is weary, and to pierce to the depth of spirit, to enfold with His love and send forth in the power of His Spirit. We must pray that He will illumine our minds so that we may choose a word that is timely and fitting and will prove of real blessing.

Individual banners

When making banners for ourselves, we usually choose texts that have spoken to us. They are words that are alive and real because they have met our need.

Banners for other people

When we make banners for other people, we seek the Lord for the Word that is right for that person.

Banners for a group or a church

Here the need is to find the Word that the Lord has for the people and so we prayerfully discuss each assignment. We decide the text in one of three ways:

1. The text is given with a request for a banner. A friend wanted a banner made for a house-church. She had several verses which she knew were right and she came along to the group for the evening to help us select a few words from these.

2. Somebody may have suggested a suitable text for a new banner. Meeting together, the group has prayed and considered these words to see if we agree. Recently I have twice

taken along what I thought were appropriate texts, but they were not required! One speaker had independently chosen the very text we had illustrated. We acknowledge that the Lord leads us very clearly in the choice of His Word and it really does become a rallying point and a standard for His people.

3. We sometimes meet without any preconceived words or designs. We state the purpose for which we've come together, and spend some time in extempore or silent prayer. We then meditate on the task and eventually scriptures come to mind, sometimes just one clear word. We then have an hour discussing ideas and words, designs and colours. We usually finish with some definite ideas and come to the next meeting able to start the background and design letters. Two to seven practical sessions follow.

The number of words

These can vary from one word such as 'Rejoice', 'Come', 'Go', and two or three such as 'Fear not', 'Jesus lives' or 'Follow Me' to a much larger number. Up to about seven words can be written in large letters. A longer sentence can be made but then the letters used should be lower case and not capitals so that the writing can be read easily. It is very important that the words should be in a colour that shows clearly against the background.

Why a group?

It is valuable to work with others on projects. In a special way the Holy Spirit guides and inspires two or three or more who meet together. His gifts are for each other and for building up his church and are not primarily for use in isolation.

Several principles emerge

1. Prayer is answered when two or three pray in Jesus' name.
2. The different abilities of the group go to make a rich and more varied whole.

3. The ideas of one person can be confirmed and checked by others. Ideas can be sifted, worked out and sometimes rejected.

4. Talents and skills are developed as we appreciate and encourage one another. Sometimes abilities emerge that one never realized one possessed.

5. One learns to give and take, to overcome fears and lack of confidence, to forgo cherished ideas in the interests of the group and to grow in confidence and love.

6. People working together as a group have fellowship and fun and share and discuss many topics as they stitch and stick.

Where?

On walls, below the lectern or pulpit, on a movable screen; as a flag hung above or to the side, on pillars, in the entrance or side-chapel, about the choir or orchestra or hung from music stands; in a Sunday school or Bible class room; in schools and colleges, playgroups and homes, hospitals and community halls; carried in processions.

When?

At festivals, family and guest services; at communion services and missionary meetings; at women's groups and evangelistic services; When a visual aid is required; at any time to aid meditation and prayer, praise and worship; when a certain scripture is meaningful and relevant to the situation or group; when outdoor rallies and Christian processions take place.

Shape and size

A large building demands a banner clearly visible from the back. Home banners can vary from a sizeable wall hanging to a tiny banner for a kitchen or child's bedroom. First decide upon the pole fittings, trimmings and shape, allowing for generous turnings at the top. Then work out the measurements and finally the design.

The space available may determine the banner shape. It is

essential to choose a shape that enhances the design and lettering; some shapes may emphasise the meaning. A festive theme might merit an elaborate shape with a fringe and perhaps tassels. A serious subject or an everyday banner could use a simple shape.

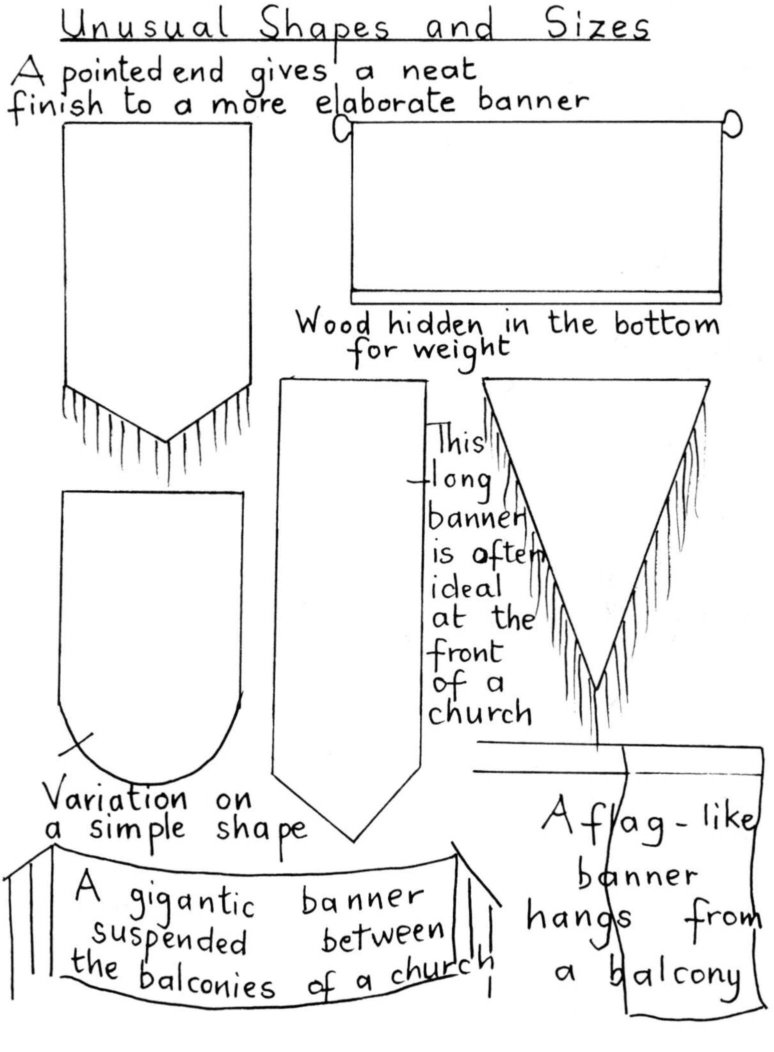

The meaning of colour in worship

Blue is the sky colour, the colour of the heavens. It stands for divinity and grace. It speaks of the infinite, eternal, unchangeable nature of the divine Son of God.

Green is the colour of growing things and speaks of life.

Yellow is the colour of promise, the future, heaven, joy and celebration.

White stands for purity and joy and celebration. Jesus was wearing white when He was transfigured on the mountain.

Red represents the passion and death of Christ and is the colour of atonement and sacrifice. It is also the colour of the earth. Adam was a son of the earth and Christ took on an earthly nature.

Purple is a royal colour. The natural colour is very rare and only recently has it been possible to use it commercially. It is the colour traditionally worn by kings and rulers. Both Mark and John describe the cloak that was mockingly thrown around Christ as a purple robe.

Black can represent sin and death, though in the ancient Egypt black was the colour of the resurrection.

Browns and *greys* convey the past, the autumn of the year and of life.

Gold is symbolic of divine righteousness. It speaks of Kingship and majesty, of glory and of heaven.

Choosing colours for an individual banner

This can be a highly individual thing, some people preferring bright definite colours, others choosing softer muted shades. Décor will obviously limit the choice of colour.

Blues and greens have a restful effect though blue can be a cold colour, particularly in a north room. Bright reds and yellows are attractive to some but others find them loud and disturbing.

Colour communicating contrasting moods

Two contrasting ranges of colour communicate very different emotions and states of being in this banner of a prison cell. The grey velvet background and black bars convey restriction, limitation and hopelessness. The brightness of the coloured letters are evocative of freedom, joy and life. This design took several weeks to evolve. A 19″ hardboard square was cut and covered with grey velvet stretched across the back by a criss-cross of strong thread. The bars were long pieces of black felt rolled and stitched before being secured both back and front. The banner was made for Ray who became an elder of our church and the words were given to me as a commission for him on the day of his induction.

Symbolism and colour on a Good Friday banner

(See colour photograph 6)

'God was in Christ reconciling the world unto Himself.' This banner on the great theme of reconciliation was made for Lent 1978.

The circular arrangement of the words convey the eternal nature of God. The circle and cross suggest the breaking in of God in Christ to redeem man into the completeness of His own nature and plan. A visit to Iona inspired the Celtic cross and much later we discovered that this cross stands for love and eternity. I brought the original idea to the group, they approved it but helped to arrange the words slightly differently and together we decided on the colours.

Grey for the cross was a link with the Celtic stone. Green was chosen as the best background for the cross and red for the letters. Much later I learnt that green symbolises life and growth and red the humanity of Christ.

The cross was quilted in grey machine stitching on a shiny grey lining material over a piece of old blanket. The pattern of the stitching was a simple adaptation of the patterns on the Iona crosses. The quilting was pinned and tacked first with the blanket between two layers of lining.

In the centre of the cross are three circles, representing the Trinity and made with beads and sequins. It is questionable whether the glitter was necessary but I'd just discovered the art of using sequins and was enjoying stitching them on in profusion!

On the Sunday in Lent when the banner was hung, John, who was to preach, shared his text for Good Friday. Whilst abroad on his job, he had prayed about the sermon in the quiet of his hotel room and had become sure he should speak on 'God was in Christ reconciling the world unto himself'. You can imagine our mutual delight that those words were already hanging underneath the pulpit! John used it as a visual aid during his talk and two other people preached on it that Easter.

The simple shape and attractive lettering accentuate the beauty of the words and their meaning.
Revelation 5:12

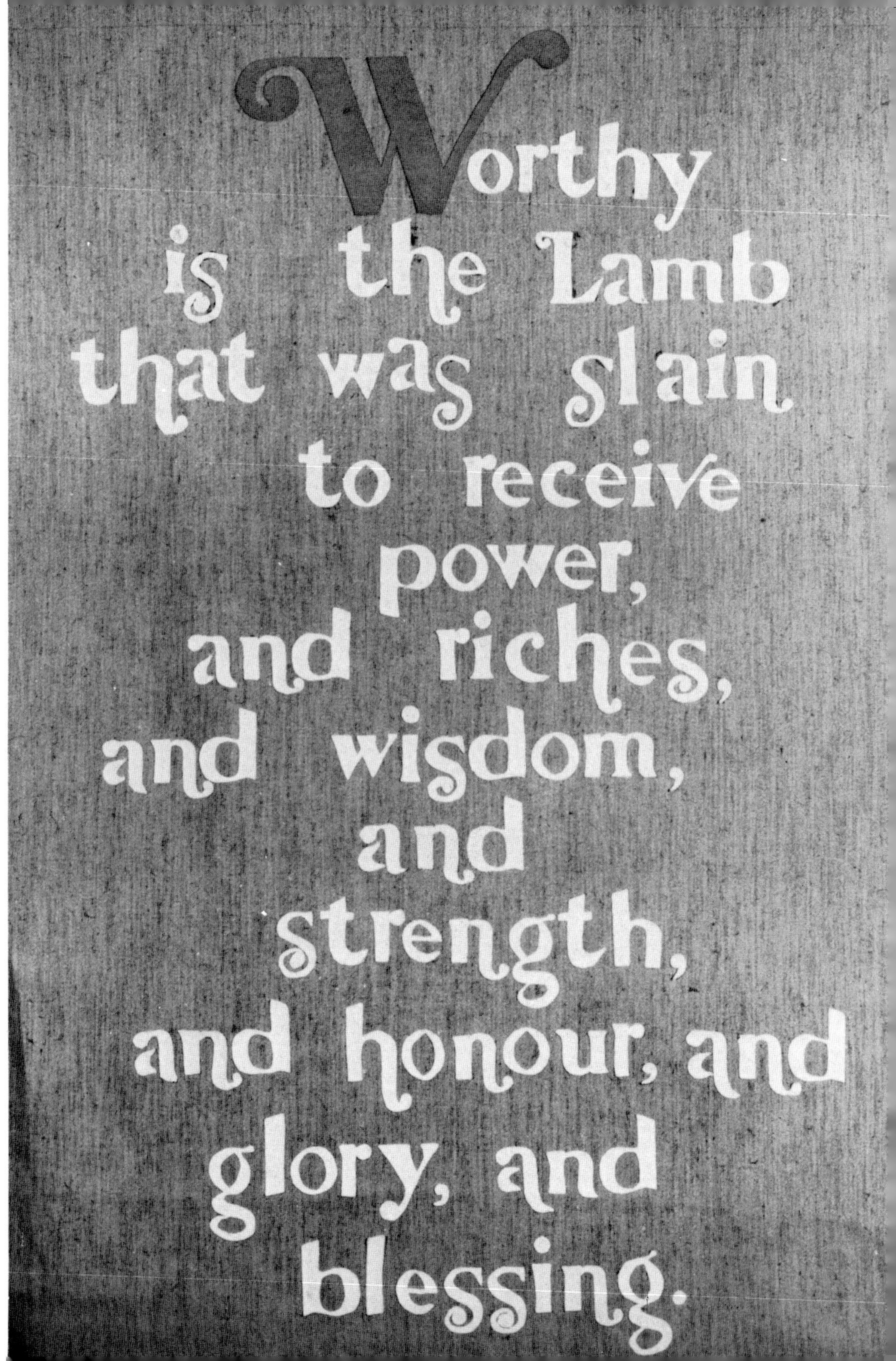
Worthy
is the Lamb
that was slain
to receive
power,
and riches,
and wisdom,
and
strength,
and honour, and
glory, and
blessing.

Squaring-up a Design

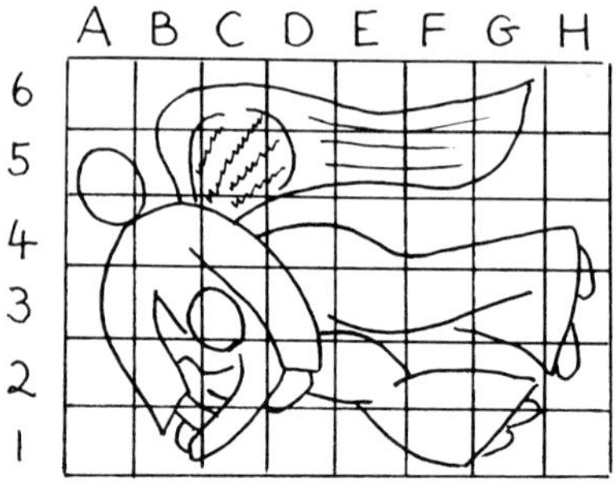

Using any ruler draw squares over your design. Draw the squares again 2 or 3 times the size. Copy your design square by square onto the larger squares.

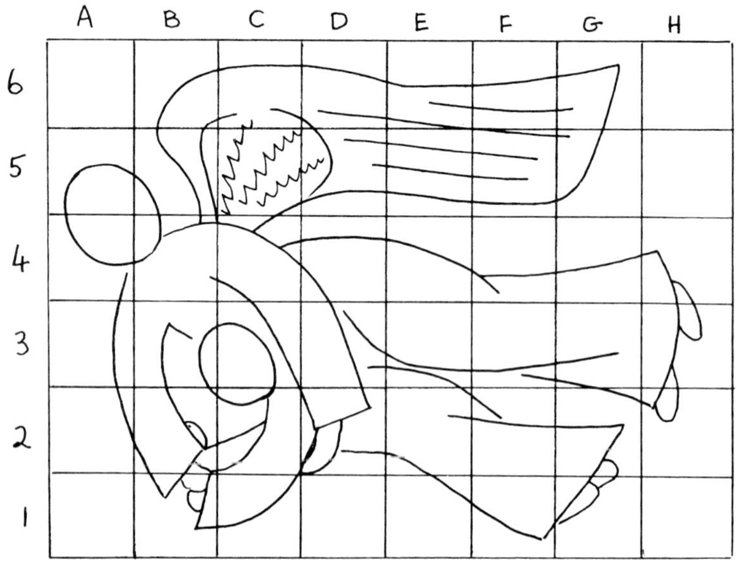

Designing banners

Some designs come in a moment. Others take weeks to mature. On occasions when no design seems relevant it could be best to leave the word to speak alone. The design should enhance the value of the words and should be part of a whole. Sometimes a design can be more meaningful without words (see Banners without words, p.14).

Make small sketches on paper and then a full-scale drawing of your intended piece. White shelf paper is suitable for this but almost any paper could be used. Enlarge your design free-hand or square it up (see diagram). Transfer the design either by using carbon or by cutting the shapes of the design out and drawing round them.

Everyone should be given the opportunity to try designing. Pencils and paper should be available at the planning sessions.

Inspiration for design

In making a banner for Discoverers, our junior-age Sunday School, we adapted a book illustration. We asked ourselves what would the Lord most want these children to know. We soon agreed that He would, above all other things, want them to know that He loved them. We decided to have a design of Jesus with a child and we traced and enlarged a picture to get these figures. The design seemed just right for the words and was later to prove of great significance to Beryl, a mother and teacher at Discoverers.

Her ten-year-old son Nigel was knocked off his bicycle and was unconscious for six days. The Lord gave Marjorie the words 'His banner over me is love' and we made them into a little banner of the same materials and colours we had chosen for the Discoverers' banner. We were glad we could make this for the family to comfort and strengthen them. When Nigel died it was hung at the service and has been in their home ever since.

Beryl returned a month later to Discoverers and during a

time of praise and singing she had a vision of the Lord with his left arm round Nigel. She had no idea that there was a banner made (which was brought a week later) showing Jesus with his left arm round a boy of similar age to Nigel.

Another clear example of God's leading was that Marjorie felt that she would like to use the reverse side of the material used for the Discoverers' banner for Beryl's banner. The Discoverers' banner was matt green slub silk curtain material. The reverse was a brighter emerald green with a silky finish. Later Marjorie realised the significance of this choice of fabric. Nigel was on the reverse side; he was in Glory and his life on earth was finished. As Nigel was now on the other side, it was most appropriate to have made the banner on the reverse side of the material. He had crossed from being a Discoverer in this life to being a Discoverer in the next.

Lettering

1. Usually non-fussy simple letters are best. It is very difficult to do elaborate small letters. Keep decorative letters for special reqirements such as imitation old manuscripts (see photos in 'Struggle to Create').

2. Choose appropriate lettering. A celebration banner might have fun letters displayed in an irregular way. A banner for Good Friday or another solemn occasion may require more formal letters.

3. If there are a number of words it is recommended to do them in lower case letters, as these can be read more easily at a distance than capitals.

4. Decide on the layout. Choose either a symmetrical or an unequally spaced layout to fit the design. Keep the layout simple and clear. Aim to communicate the idea or message rather than draw too much attention to the letters unless the words are to stand alone, in which case you may wish to make them more decorative.

5. Sources for letters can be lettering in newspapers or magazines, posters, greeting cards and prayer cards, etc. Several books are available on lettering and it is well worth

HIS BANNER OVER
ME
IS
LOVE

getting one. The Letraset book is a mine of ideas and you can buy it from an art shop.

6. Draw out letters on exercise, graph or dress-making paper. The shape of an 'O' can be used to help you draw a 'b', 'd', 'p', etc. Keep your letters in envelopes for future use.

7. Cut out by pinning paper letters on to felt or non-fraying materials. It is possible to cut out several identical letters at once.

8. Many of our letters have been glued on but after a year or two the glue can show through felt letters. We use a latex-based glue. We still continue to stick on letters for more instant banners but would recommend stitching if at all possible.

9. Letters can be fastened to material by doing a running stitch down the middle of the letters and so fixing them on. This is an excellent quick way for all types of letters. Chain stitch can also be embroidered down the centre to give a pleasant effect. Letters can also be sewn on round the edges.

10. Cord or thread can be sewn on with matching or invisible thread.

11. Don't make heavy work of the sewing by tackling it too meticulously but have a light touch and work quickly with as large stitches as you think possible.

Bold lettering and design

Bold letters are very suitable for banners made on old screens. The size and strength of letters do justice to the words; emphasising the importance of the message and making the words clearly visible at a distance. The basis of the screen can be thin hardboard and coloured card or paper can be used for the letters.

Material for banners

Should all banners be made to last?

There are no hard and fast rules. Paper and card may make an attractive banner but in time will become worn; they are ideal for a banner that will only be used for one or two occasions. The aesthetic value can be equal to a more elaborate banner made out of silk and embroidered threads and will take a fraction of the time.

Banners made to last are best made from material. It gives the works and design a more enduring quality and these banners will last in good condition for a number of years.

How do you know what material to use?

For the majority of banners plain materials are best; velvet and silk are best kept for weddings or for banners of detailed, rich,work. It is hard work stitching felt letters onto velvet. For a quick simple design cheap fabrics or hessian are appropriate; for a more enduring banner choose cotton, linen or curtain fabric or other fabrics of a similar quality. Make sure the material is firm enough to hang properly. Both background and figures may be strengthened by iron-on vilene.

Where can you obtain materials?

The best source of background fabrics is found at the remnant counter of a curtain fabric shop. There is often a good selection of materials at reasonable prices. Friends may be able to supply old curtains and jumble sales may produce some useful finds.

Does it matter which way the material hangs?

Cotton and woven materials and dull and plain fabrics can be hung any way and their surfaces appear the same. Pile fabrics such as velvet appear darker or lighter than they really are when placed certain ways. Shot silks change depending on the way the fabric is hung. The full beauty and character of any material can be judged best from a distance.

Where do you keep the materials?

Odd pieces collected by a group may fill several boxes and it is good if these can be stored in a central place, but if not, in the homes of members. Material can be bought as each banner is planned. It is also advisable to have several pieces of plain fabric in hand that go well in the church. Material required should be ordered well in advance.

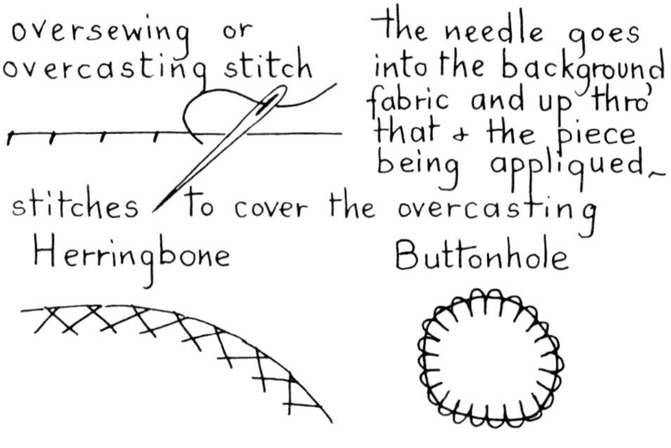

Appliqué and embroidery

Appliqué

Appliqué is the art of sewing shapes of material onto a background. It produces clear and simple decoration and covers large areas quickly.

'Alleluia' banner

Red, orange and brown cotton materials, two patterned and one plain were used for this very simple banner, made for a Nigerian Sunday School. The figures were enlarged from an illustration in the Good News Bible. These drawings were cut out to make patterns and pinned on the materials, cut out and arranged on the background fabric. As the cotton materials frayed easily they were sewn on with small neat oversewing stitches of the same colour. For an extra finish blanket stitch, back stitch, herringbone or couching could be used around the edge. Couching with silk cord or inexpensive piping is an attractive way to give a definite outline to a shape on a banner.

Appliqué using machine and hand embroidery

Tree Banner (See colour photograph 9)

This design evolved after much discussion and arranging and rearranging of fabrics, cords and threads. Perhaps the meaning of the picture is best found in Psalm 1. It is without words so it may be wide open to individual interpretation.

The leaves were designed first. The basic shape was cut out in seven or so different green felts. The next step was discovered by Margaret experimenting on her sewing-machine and using a zig-zag stitch to fasten a larger shape of green or yellow net on to the felt shape. She added a central vein with another stitch. In most of the net shapes the centre has been cut out. Later, when the whole was nearly complete the leaves were carefully arranged and glued into place on the background of silvery grey curtain fabric. Small clusters of cherries

Details of Machine and Hand Embroidery on the Tree Design

Basic leaf shape in felt-net cut in leaf shape but larger and with centre removed

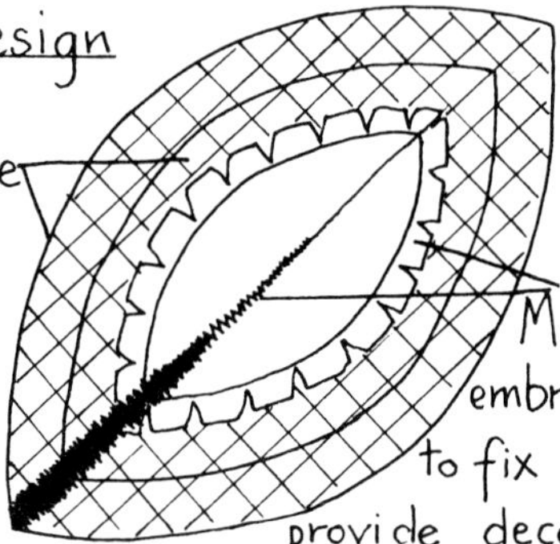

Machine embroidery to fix net & provide decoration.

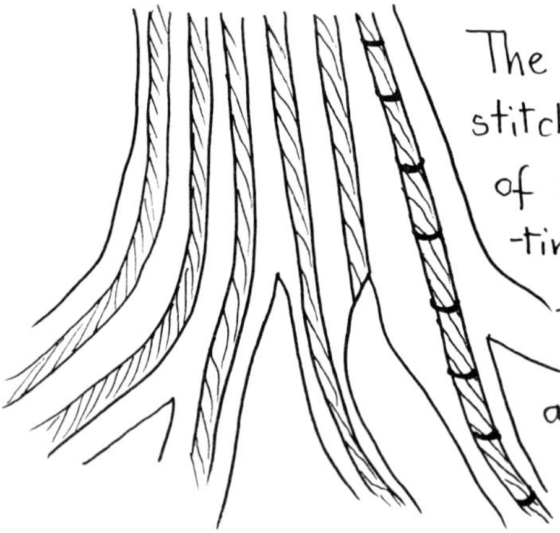

The bark is made by stitching, one by one, lengths of brown & cream knit-ting wool onto the felt shape of the tree trunk. Couching, a simple short stitch, holds the wool in place.

The net is held in place by a stab stitch, a small stitch where the thread comes from behind, goes over a thread of net and returns behind the fabric and along to the next stitch.

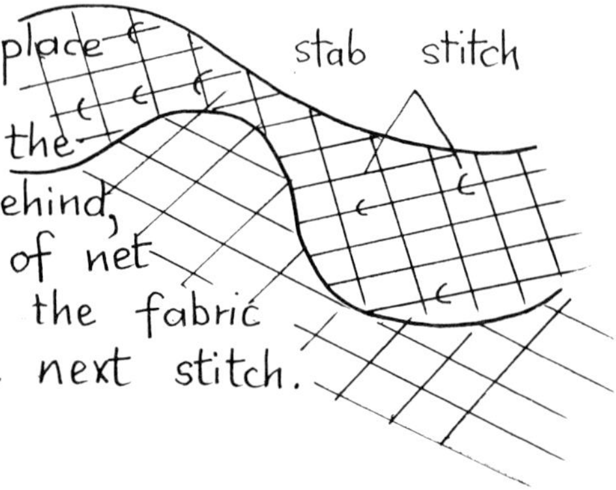

Photograph 1 St Michael-le-Belfrey. Made during a renewal week after meditation on the words 'we have this treasure in earthern vessels'. The coins and jewels are made from coloured and silvery papers with bright ribbons and sequins.

57" x 30"

Photograph 2 Made from gold and coloured papers with various printed pictures, each representing a name of Jesus. *Left to right:* Saviour, Lion, Lamb, Bright and Morning Star, Light of the World, the Vine, Alpha and Omega, King of Kings.

Photograph 3 Stained by tea leaves, the reverse side of this piece of wallpaper gives the effect of an ancient manuscript. The letters, made of paper, have been stuck on.

Photograph 4 Sunflowers are made to look real by raising the centre of the flower and using loose petals. Sunflowers always face the sun reminding us that we should turn our hearts towards the Son of God.

54" x 24"

Photograph 5
The symbols of God's sovereignty are beautifully set against green velvet on this banner made for the home. The words affirm faith in the greatness, majesty and wisdom of the Lord.

Photograph 6 Made for Easter, this banner has been hung in a permanent position in another church. The red letters symbolize the blood of Christ and the green the hill of Calvary. The grey Celtic cross inspired the design.

47" square

Photograph 7 The text was our inspiration for the design of this Christmas banner. The message of the banner reminds us that because God came down to man, the way is open for man to go up to God.

35" x 5

Photograph 8 This simple banner was made by Jenny at her father's request. It hung in his bedroom in the short time before he stepped into the reality that to die is to gain.

Photograph 9 This banner was designed to hang permanently in church. A tree can stand alone as a design because each person interprets different Scriptural meanings. Consider Psalm 1.

45" x 53"

Photograph 10
St Michael-le-Belfrey. Four and five-year-old children drew this banner under the leadership of Shirley who had taught them that Jesus is with them. The children were asked to do a drawing of themselves doing some of the things they enjoyed. They then stuck the shapes of material that were cut for them on to the paper drawings and these were glued to hessian.

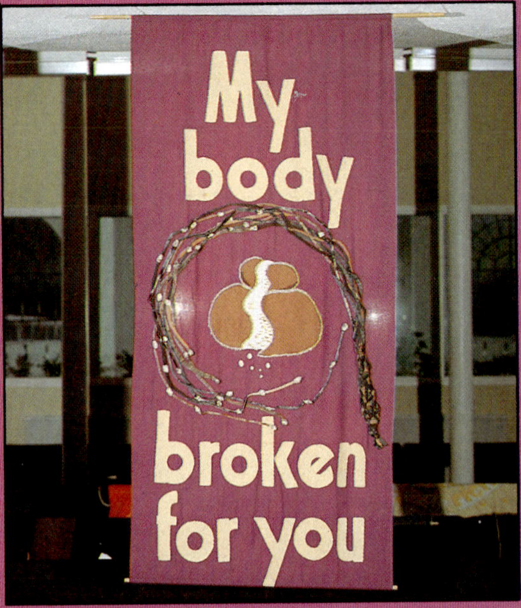

Photograph 11
St Michael-le-Belfrey. This is one of four banners used at communion services. Purple represents royalty and the whiplash was made from leather strips and milk bottle tops. The bread was made from felt and cord.

Photograph 12 St Michael-le-Belfrey. The flowers on this Easter banner are attached with running and oversewing stitches. The three-dimensional letters of this great affirmation in Colossians 1:27, are made from shiny surfaced materials.

Photograph 13 St Michael-le-Belfrey. The text is taken from Isaiah which includes the promise of God to pour water onto the thirsty land and streams on the dry ground. Water symbolizes the Holy Spirit.

were stitched into place. The tree trunk and roots were cut out in beige felt and different shades of brown and cream knitting wool were couched into lines to form the bark of the tree.

The water took much adjusting and positioning of coloured nets and lengths of cord before it was pleasing to the eye. The nets were placed first and when held in position were pinned and then couched in place. One green cord was added to reflect the green of the tree and a bank of green net was stitched above the water. The net was double thickness to give enough strength of colour.

Other techniques

Card and paper. We have made a few banners from paper and card, shiny paper and magazine pictures. Three are illustrated in this book; Easter posters on p. 55, *Wonderful Counsellor* and *Jesus* (in colour). These are difficult to store and usually do not last in a good condition for very long. However they can be very attractive for the occasion for which they are made and cost very little. Although we choose to do mainly appliqué banners on material here are some alternative ideas.

String. A superb arrangement of Noah and his animals was done in different coloured strings; some string had been dyed or painted and some left natural. The string was glued on piece by piece to follow the animals' body shapes.

Batik. The design was done in batik, using dyes and wax-resist and words were added embroidered in chain stitch.

Tissue. Tiny balls of rolled-up tissue were glued all over the design on to a primed hardboard background. Then the design was painted. A picture of the crucifixion was done this way and the result was very clear and bold.

Collage. Last August I made a cameo of a corner of a field with ears of wheat and artificial poppies and daisies. They were stitched on to a blue material background and the white letters in the sky said 'Ripe for harvest'.

Choice of Banners

How do we decide which banner to put up each Sunday? We have two or three semi-permanent ones that are relevant on all occasions. We change these three or four times a year.

We put other banners up for one to six weeks. These are more immediate ones, some being made in two sessions. We also have a list of all the banners available so that the leaders in our fellowship can illustrate a sermon or a service.

As this book goes to print half our congregation is meeting on Sunday mornings in a local school as we have grown too big as a fellowship for one building. Those of us in the school are taking banners and hanging them up just for each service. We keep the majority of the banners folded in a cupboard at my home. Ideally a safe place should be set aside at the church. Some banners we use belong to individuals and we borrow them from time to time. We have given a few banners away, mostly to friends overseas.

This small banner 11¾ in × 15 in (30 x 38 cm) was made for two friends from our church who are on the missionary ship *Doulos*. On the reverse side is a path leading to a cross and the words 'Come unto Me'.

Banners in processions

Ideas

1. A board painted with household paint.
2. A flag or banner made of different appliquéd materials.
3. Fabric paint on material.
4. A card one which would just last one wet occasion.

Processional banners can be simply lettering or design with lettering. The quality must be good. Shoddy work and paints that run do not enhance the cause for which the banners are made. Calico can be used as a backing for a really strong banner and it will prevent the light showing through.

A festive decorative medieval feeling can be given by bells and tassels. Few and bold words are best. Contrasting colours show up designs and letters.

A successful banner was made by Angela for a procession at the Feast of Tabernacles in Jerusalem

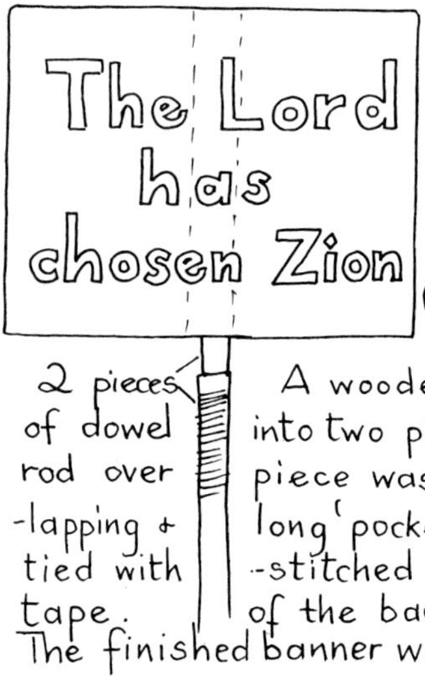

Made of cotton material & felt letters the bottom seam was left open so that a piece of polystyrene (or hardboard) could be put inside.

2 pieces of dowel rod over-lapping & tied with tape.

A wooden rod was cut into two pieces. The top piece was fitted into a long 'pocket' machined-stitched on the inside of the back of the material

The finished banner was 16"x21" 41cm x 53cm

Banners in Processions
wooden board
on a stick
Come unto Me
decorative flag
banner in
appliqué of materials.
JESUS IS ALIVE
Gigantic banner of cheap
colourful materials.

Power in the Word

by Marjorie Harris

'Would you like to join the banner group?' I was excited at the thought and I loved the Word of God, but I didn't know how to go about collage, let alone the many different techniques our banner-making might call forth! I felt I should seek the Lord about it, as if the call was from Him, He would enable me and show it wasn't just a sewing circle I was joining! I read in Isaiah 62, verses 10 and 11, 'Go through, go through the gates, prepare the way for the people; build up, build up the highway, clear it of stones, lift up an ensign over the peoples. Behold the Lord has proclaimed to the end of the earth: Say to the daughter of Zion 'Behold your salvation comes.' I realised that banners could lift up the Lord, comfort His people and praise His Name—and so I joined the group. We have found in the group great blessing in the making of banners as they have come out of our worship and have been a way of expressing ourselves to Him.

My first banner was made to praise the Lord when our daughter was five months old and made a miraculous recovery from a serious illness. The Lord promised she would be brought back from the brink of the grave (Psalm 30) and at the eleventh hour the surgeon operated successfully and saved her life. I made a small triangular white banner out of material from my wedding dress and embroidered it in red with the words 'Glory to the Lord' and hung it above her cot.

I am very fond of what I call my 'instant banners'. I put the Word of God on to a card with felt-tips and keep it close at hand for the Lord to minister through during the day. At the moment the current one is propped up against the washing-up liquid. Others are on a little notice board in the kitchen.

The essence of banners is the Word of God. We must not boast of our work. Our aim is to seek the Lord for His Word and lift Him up that He may draw people to Himself.

The diary of a banner

(See colour photograph 5)

Beryl wanted a banner that she could hang on her living room wall. She was impressed by the words 'Our God Reigns' when she first heard a song with these words in the chorus. Several months later she saw the same words outside a Dorset village church and knew they were the exact ones she wanted.

Early January, 1978. Five of us met in Marjorie's living room. Beryl told us the words and why she had chosen them. We then had a time of prayer and worship, thinking about God as King. We prayed that the Lord would guide us that evening to make something beautiful that would glorify Him.

Next we questioned Beryl on her ideas. She wanted a soft green that would blend in with her living room. Moving on to discuss a design that would symbolise the King, we looked at a book about the Queen's coronation. We were interested to discover that the cross and the orb are symbolic of Christianity reigning over the world. Marjorie pointed out that, in the Bible, the significance of gold represents God's sovereignty and the testing of our faith is compared to the refining of gold.

We decided to make the orb, sceptre and crown by stretching gold fabric over stiff card (old cereal boxes). It was a pleasant change to be using beautiful materials, because we had been working on backgrounds of old curtains or hessian and someone had been overheard to remark: 'not another old piece of sacking!' We then drew up a list of shopping.

Late January 1978. Beryl brought a remnant of green velvet found at a furnishing fabric shop. We decided the way the pile should lie to catch the light most effectively, marked it with pins, not having any tailors' chalk, and cut it out to measure 14 in × 20 in (35 × 51 cm).

Beryl cut an old blouse of gold lurex to cover the orb, cross and sceptre. Allowing for a generous overlap, we glued the wrong side of the shaped card with quick-sticking glue round the edge and pulled the material over on to the tacky glue. An old bracelet with small stones was sewn across the circumference of the orb.

Early February. Beryl's husband John had made the crown at home using gold and purple and white fur and had added the jewels. The only colour that seemed right for the letters, was white, so these were cut out.

Late February. Marjorie had made three flat tabs of the velvet material, and tacked them to the top on the reverse side, covering the back with a piece of lining material. The banner was hung in the bathroom so the steam could erase any creases. The objects were sewn on with invisible nylon thread. The letters were sewn on by hand.

March. The banner was hung on a brass curtain rod on two brass supports John fixed to the living room wall. The total effect was one of great richness and splendour.

Beryl says the words have given her strength and help during a very sad and difficult family time, and that the banner has been a constant reminder, even in the darkest moments, that 'Our God Reigns'. Lent to the church, it has also been the theme of many meditations, praise and worship.

Rejoice in the Lord

by Evelyn Lucus

(See colour photograph 4)

I came to the banner workshop with an open mind aware that I needed to listen to the Lord for the idea for a banner for my home. I knew I must work the idea out in such a way that it would have an aesthetic value and my family could identify with the design and words.

When I first saw the brown velvet lying among other remnants on the table, in my mind's eye I saw sunflowers and the words 'Rejoice in the Lord'. I decided to design each section to give a 3D effect.

Paper flowers and letters were placed to give a right balance. The attempt was rather disastrous until my children suggested I go outside and look at a real sunflower; this made a great improvement. It was important to really know how the leaf grew on the stalk and its size and behaviour. Each petal and leaf has rows of back-stitching in different shades of green and yellow to represent the veins.

The letters are fawn felt and each one has a row of chain-stitching down the centre in the colours of the sunflower; the dots have filled-in centres of brown embroidery thread. The flower centres are made of padded felt stitched all over with elongated french knots. Both leaves and petals are only lightly stitched, so that they appear to stand out from the background. The letters tend to slip on the velvet but with prayer and patience I managed to stitch them on by hand.

The banner has become a daily celebration of who I am in the Lord. 'Rejoice' always speaks to me of something much deeper than superficial happiness. One of its meanings is 'to be blessed in the possession of'. This is a marvellous description of our standing as Christians. We are blessed in the possession of Christ, His love and faithfulness. Therefore we can have a confidence, a sure and certain hope concerning our present and future, which is always centred in Christ. This is where the sunflower comes in. Wherever you plant sunflowers they will always turn their heads to face the sun. Reaching for the sunshine, they absorb it and mature, their large bright heads are bursting with food and nourishment for others in sunflower oil and seeds. As we turn our faces to Jesus He changes us into His likeness; He is the finisher, the perfecter, the maturer of our faith.

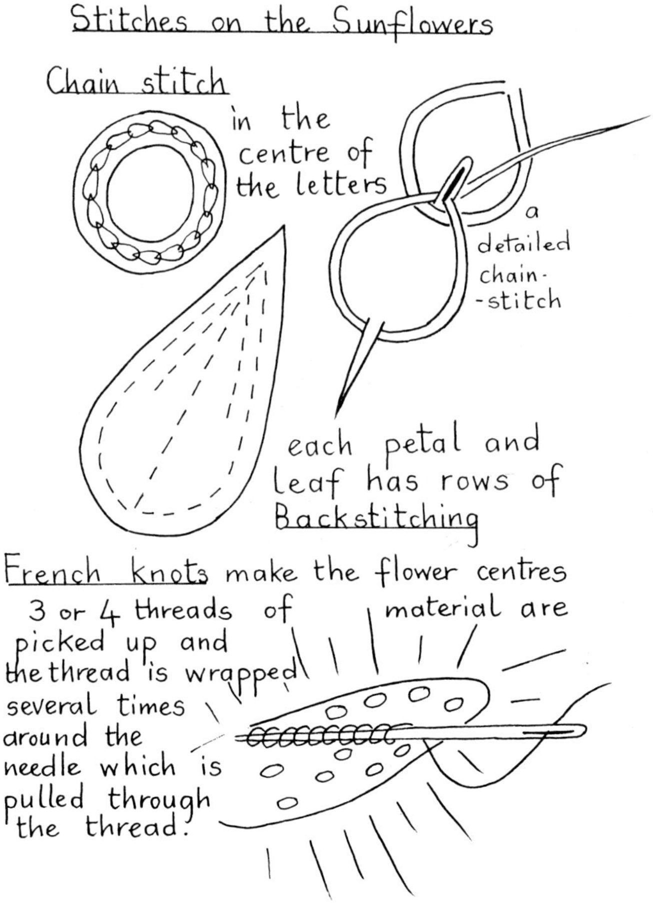

Struggle to create

(See colour photographs 2 and 3)

The struggle produced between the germ of an idea and its final out-working can be called creative tension. The tension in banner-making comes when one takes the initial concept and tries to work it out in terms of material, whether fabric, paper or some other medium.

Marjorie and I were the only two at that planning session for the Christmas banners. However, we were sure of the words. We had pondered on them for two weeks and our pastor, Stuart, had independently suggested them. 'Great big mediaeval manuscripts,' he said, 'the words Wonderful Counsellor, Mighty God, Everlasting Father and Prince of Peace.' He'd scribbled away to show us a sketch. 'Get out a library book about illuminated letters—Lindisfarne Gospels, Book of Kells.' Reflecting on these great words of Isaiah, we decided on four parchment-like scrolls.

Next came the episode of the tea-leaves. You may wonder what damp, used tea-leaves have to do with banner-making. They are an invaluable aid to the making of the parchment-type background. Marjorie asked friends in her house-group to save their used tea-leaves, and one Sunday morning hung a bucket bag outside church with a little notice saying 'For Tea-Leaf Offerings'. A space was cleared in my spare bedroom and masses of newspaper spread over the floor. We rolled out lengths of wallpaper, approximately two metres long. We spread the leaves thoroughly all over the five sheets of paper and left them scattered like this to dry. Two days later I went to remove the leaves and find underneath the ancient parchment finish, but, alas, the tea-leaves stuck fast to what I realised must have been pre-pasted vinyl! A few more sheets were easily prepared.

The busier you are, the more you need to pray, so, conscious of the task ahead, I got myself down to the women's prayer meeting. Sharing our need for inspiration, I said that we were undertaking to do these illuminated letters, the originals of which took monks a life-time. When the prayer time concluded, Katie, an American lady, with a degree in Art, and Vicky (a Bible College student) offered to join us. We all went back to my place and started working on the letters. Marjorie worked on the lower case letters and the rest on capitals. Katie completed four of the eight letters. We all took work home to continue during the week.

It was my task to work on the name 'Jesus'. I found this to be the greatest source of joy of any creative task I have ever undertaken, but it was also a spiritual struggle. All the week I'd had a sense of heaviness, and on the following evening, Wednesday, I was so unhappy I went to talk to a friend called Ruth. Explaining to her the project, I suggested this cloud on my spirit was an attack from the powers of darkness because I was working on the name 'Jesus'. She said this could be likely because the Bible promises that if Jesus is lifted up He will draw all men unto Himself, and that the power in the raising of His name could be hated by the enemy. She prayed for deliverance and protection. I returned to continue the task, still struggling but with the weight on my spirit gone.

We decided that the name 'Jesus' should be in capitals, so I cut these out in large pale yellow paper letters. Plain gold-coloured letters, made of thin card, identical in shape but slightly smaller, were placed on top of each yellow letter, so allowing a contrasting border to show. Trying to invent some decoration around and inside the letters, I cut up old Christmas cards to see if these would fit. Suddenly, after long hours, an idea came into my mind of representing the names of Jesus pictorially. Inspiration from the Lord can sometimes be so clear and can come from outside yourself when you have no ideas within. As I continued I had a sense of standing apart, watching the idea grow.

I did not have the ability to paint the pictures required, but I did have several printed pictures. I had recently bought a greeting card of a lion's head; this would represent the Lion of the Tribe of Judah. The regal yet warm face of the lion was closely linked in my mind with the Aslan of C. S. Lewis'

GLORY
TO THE
LORD

books. The picture fitted into the upper part of the letter 'e'. Below it fitted a picture of a lamb taken from a Ladybird book. A photograph of Earth taken from the moon provided 'The Light of the World', and one of the night sky with a silver star added was 'The Bright and Morning Star'. A poster of a vine was slipped into the centre of the 'u'. The 'J' provided a niche for the picture of the Saviour in the manger. The last letter remained. I cut a yellow card 'Alpha' and 'Omega' and also a red and gold crown for the two parts of the 's'.

The pleasure of doing this remained with me for days. The near esctasy of knowing the inspiration came from the Lord and yet being His mind and hands for the outworking of it, was the greatest joy in anything I have ever made.

The next evening Marjorie and I completed and assembled the words. When David, Marjorie's husband, returned from a half-night of prayer, we were still working and he was in time to give us his usual benediction!

The overwhelming impression of the Carol Service was one of joy. With new carpets and chairs, flowers and banners, song and carols backed by a mini-orchestra and sung by a packed church, it was a beautiful evening. David summed it all up for me when he said, 'How much the Lord must have enjoyed tonight, because we'd done it all for Him.'

This colourful banner with a red poppy on a cream background was made quickly to use in the summer for Sunday worship.

Children's banner competition

This competition took place a month before Easter 1979. Boys and girls between the ages of 5-18 were asked to submit a design for an Easter banner. They were given as much freedom as possible, with just the following guidelines.

Design your banner:

1. Any size or shape.
2. Any material.
3. Keep it simple.
4. You may have help with the figure drawing from adults or copy figures from books or Bibles.
5. Submit a drawing. Colour it or indicate colours you want.

The entries

We were handed fifteen drawings and one finished banner. Since each one was done with thought and care we decided to make them all. Three designs we chose to enlarge considerably to hang at the front of the church. We decided the others could be fairly small so that, if the children wished, they could hang them afterwards in their bedrooms.

Twelve banners

We divided the smaller banners between members of the group. At home we enlarged them and cut shapes out in felt in the colours that the children had suggested. We used hessian for the background and fringed the edges. We all used the same set of capital letters. Most of us were able to visit the children to help them stick the designs and words.

Finally pieces of flat rod were glued to the top of each piece of hessian and a cord was tied on each end.

Three banners

Jo Gibbons, Claire Reid and Clare McFiggin came on Monday evenings to work with our help, on the larger banners.

Jo—*'He is risen'*

Jo made up her design almost exactly to the pattern and colours she had originally planned. We cut a large piece of hessian which we laid over newspaper on the floor and Jo glued on to it a royal blue cotton sky and stuck different overlapping patches of green hillside below. She chose yellow material to go behind the central cross and fringed it to suggest rays of light. The large plain capital letters were a similar yellow but they were cut out in felt. Margery made a substantial rolled-away stone and stitched some grey felt around the entrance to the cave, ruckling it up to give a rocky effect. Finally the empty grave-clothes, little pieces of folded sheet were gently stitched in position.

Claire—*'He is risen—Glory'*

Claire Reid's drawing showed the joy of Easter morning in a Christian rejoicing in His Risen Lord. We copied a joyous leaping figure and it was done in the dark blue colour Claire suggested. She had previously hemmed a pale blue linen background and on to this was drawn the figure squared up from the original. The blue cord was sewn on to suggest arms and legs. Silver ribbon letters were cut and Claire stuck them together and an older Clare stuck them on the material.

Matthew St John and Clare McFiggin—*'It is finished'*

Seven-year-old Matthew drew a cross for the competition but didn't have any words. His parents suggested he might think of some and then he said 'It is finished'. The colours were chosen by us all. The cross was to be gold speaking of the holiness and majesty of Christ the King and the red was chosen to represent His blood and sacrificial death. The brown provided a sombre background for these bright colours.

We asked Clare McFiggin to join us to make this banner. She had the tricky job of positioning the thick cord double in the shape of a cross and she worked this out with mathematical precision. Marjorie cut out the letters and helped Clare stick them on. A red fringe and cord were added as finishing touches.

Conclusion

The children immensely enjoyed the project and took pride in seeing the finished results hanging in the church and later in the room where their 'Discoverer' Group takes place. We hope the happiness and joy this competition inspired will encourage the participants to further original creations.

JESUS
WILL GO
WITH
YOU

A wedding banner made by children

'Jesus will go with you'

This banner was made by a group of ten and eleven-year-old girls for a teacher, a colleague of mine who led a Bible Club with me in the lunch hour to which these girls came. It was made as a wedding and goodbye present when she left to get married.

The idea of the gift arose over the lunch table and in between mouthfuls of sausage and chips the girls decided the words of their picture should be 'Jesus will go with you'.

The picture was done in fabrics during several lunch hours. The design evolved step by step. The central idea was of Jesus walking as friend and guide with the bride and groom on either side into the future. A church with a cross was chosen to symbolise Christian marriage and the gaily coloured flowers represented happiness.

I helped with the drawing of the figures but the fabrics and colours of the clothes were decided on by the girls who felt that nothing else would be appropriate but to have the bride and groom, in full wedding attire complete with top and tails. The banner was presented to a surprised and delighted teacher at the last assembly of term.

A wedding banner

by Robert Parry

Many waters cannot quench love

The conception

Presented with the text from Song of Solomon 8:7, our first task was to produce a design to incorporate both these words and the theme of marriage. First we prayed asking the Lord to inspire us in our creativity and to help us produce something which could bring Him glory and displayed in their home, would constantly remind John and Lorraine of their position in the Lord.

The design

The final design was the result of several preliminary drawings; the rock and the cross together symbolising the sure foundation of the love of Christ. On the rock stand the man and the woman jointly acknowledging that love. The waves symbolise the mighty waters of life which may come but which can never quench or destroy the love of Christ for them.

Construction

A backcloth was chosen which resembled the colour of the sea; it was cut to size and hemmed. On to this were glued the rock and the figures which were made from various shades of felt. The cross was made from dark cloth and stretched and stuck round two pieces of card. The waves were two shades of blue/turquoise felt bordered with white piping. The letters were chosen, cut in felt and stuck on to the backing. Each of these tasks were shared amongst us and finally the banner was trimmed and hung in place for the wedding service.

Many waters
cannot quench
love

A banner for my father

by Jenny Bates

(See colour photograph 8)

It was back in February 1979 when we realised that the bone cancer my father was suffering from could not be controlled and he became bedridden. Having just four walls to stare at all day long he asked me to make a banner for him. The text he chose was 'For me to live is Christ, to die is gain.'

I had never attempted a banner before nor had any idea how to go about it, so I enlisted the help of two members of the design group, in particular Marjorie and Priscilla. Between us Priscilla and I chose some material in bright green and cut out the felt for the lettering in yellow and gold. In the language of colours, as I understand it, green represents physical life and gold eternal life.

Marjorie showed me how to pull away the threads at the bottom of the banner to make a fringe and I sewed on the letters by hand.

We felt a design would not only brighten up the banner but also give emphasis to the meaning of the words and the obvious choice proved to be a butterfly. I borrowed a book from the library on butterflies, traced out the shape in brown felt and embroidered orange splashes on the wings which produced a reasonably authentic Red Admiral. I used only a few stitches to put it in place as I wanted the butterfly to appear resting against the material rather than stitched closely to it.

The life-cycle of a butterfly is a wonderful miracle of nature. Out of that ugly dead pupa or chrysalis emerges a beautiful creature with delicate wings and colours. When a child of God goes to be with his Lord he leaves behind his old useless body and becomes a new creation and lovely to look at.

I completed the banner in a hurry as it seemed then that my father was slipping away so quickly I might not be in time to finish it, but of course, I was. For several months it occupied a focal spot in his room and was a source of considerable comment and question from many who visited him.

It was on August 15 that my father finally passed to be with his Lord. He had arranged some months earlier that the banner should be hung in the church at his funeral and a simple gospel message was given around the text. There are no coincidences for the Christian; on the following morning my mother read in her Daily Light, 'Christ shall be magnified in my body whether it be by life, or by death, for me to live is Christ, to die is gain.'

A visit to York

(See colour photographs 1, 10, 11, 12 and 13)

I went to York to learn from and share with the leaders of the banner group at St Michael-le-Belfrey. I had met Janet and Shirley fifteen months earlier for just a few hours and this visit was for a weekend. St Michael-le-Belfrey is a large, very old Anglican church lying in the shadow of York Minster.

On the Saturday evening Janet and I talked at length about the way the Lord has led in the banner making in both our groups. St Michael-le-Belfrey banner group express their aim as follows. 'To express the Word of God in art form in a fresh way each time we make a banner'. They also claim to make the church building more attractive, bringing a sense of celebration contributing to the message and worship of the service. They say that the visitor can walk into the church and know immediately that it is alive because of the effect of the banners, and before the service starts, people can be prepared and opened to receive in a gentle and acceptable way. They regard banners as a focal point for meditation and conveying a message from the Lord, reminding people of who God is, of His promises and lifting someone's sad heart.

All the work of making the banners had been made possible by two support groups of two or three ladies who sew banners that the design group have cut out and tacked ready for sewing.

Every Sunday morning there is family worship with the whole family attending. While I was there the talk by the rector was illustrated with the overhead projector by Shirley. The theme of the service was 'Promised by the Spirit'.

The banners were connected with the theme of the talk; one banner showed a verse about the Holy Spirit and nine other smaller banners each showed one of the fruits of the Spirit, love, joy, peace, patience, kindness, goodness, faithfulness, gentleness and self-control. The nave has large pillars each side so the banners are often made in a series and one or two

Flowers above a crown of thorns are the subject of this small banner made by one friend for another at St Michael-le-Belfrey.

large ones are hung at the front and smaller ones on the other pillars. The large banner that was up at the front showed a figure with upraised arms and upturned face ready to receive and the words above in rainbow colours mingled with pouring water were 'I will pour my Spirit upon you'. (See colour photograph 13). The rainbow colours signify the promise of God. The waters were different shades of blue net. The little banners were done in different related shades of greens, yellows, reds, purples and blues thus forming a rainbow series down the church. For instance the word patience was done in greeny-yellows. The letters were vertical, and again, pouring water made of net had been added. Janet told me that the banner had been made two years previously for Whitsun day and that the drama, singing and music groups had worked independently for the service not realising they were all expressing the same words so all the worship focused on the promise of Jesus to pour out His Spirit.

This is one of seven banners of spring flowers that accompany *Christ in you the hope of glory*.

A communion service followed the family service and one song we sang was 'Broken for me'. This theme of Christ suffering for us is shown in the banners that are sometimes hung at the communion services. (See colour photograph 11). The passion and death of Christ has moved Janet and her husband Colin, very deeply. Janet said she has come to see the Crown of Thorns as something terrible and yet at the same time, beautiful.

The banners were not as difficult to make as they seem; there is very little embroidery and milk bottle tops, leather-thonging, felt and wool are used.

Meeting Janet and Shirley and others at St Michael-le-Belfrey I came away knowing the Holy Spirit has and is continuing to give fresh and original inspiration to the group and has freed them from formality and inhibition, setting them free to express their praise and love in these rich and joyous banners.

Janet wrote the following points on the organisation of the visual arts seminar that is one of the workshops of the twice yearly St Michael-le-Belfrey renewal weeks.

1. We usually share our Christian names, the place we're from, the reason why we've come and art experience, if any.

2. Sometimes we have a time of sharing our banners or photos of them particularly ones we are in the process of making.

3. We have worship, prayer and meditation on a Bible passage which Shirley and I have already chosen and which is linked with the theme of the week.

4. We get everyone to write down (and sketch, if possible) texts, thoughts, designs, etc., and then we share them.

5. We leaders try to draw the threads together; often when we have reached the point of having a rough idea of what we want we get everyone to try to draw how they see the idea. We also encourage them to continue thinking along those lines between seminars, listening to the Lord regarding the banner.

6. During the rest of the seminars we get on with the practical, starting off by focusing on the Lord in prayer and song.

Starting a banner group

by Penny Dawson

'How about making banners?' Come and have coffee on Thursday and we'll talk about it.'

I liked the thought of visiting this particular friend, so I agreed. We, talked about banners and many other things, prayed together, and arranged to meet again the next week. During that week I wondered just where all this would lead. Where do you begin? What with? How? Perhaps I had better start with the Lord. Was there anything special He had done at that time? There was my visit to hospital for minor examination under anaesthetic. I had felt very aware of the Lord's presence and His peace surrounding me while I had been praying about that.

A week later I shared these thoughts, only to find that my friend had also been thinking of peace. The text came easily, 'My peace I give unto you'. A length of hessian served as backing. Peace comes from Jesus and is signified by a dove, so an outline of these two figures was copied from an invaluable book called 'Help, I Can't Draw' published by Falcon Books. I discovered that my friend could draw so I found myself left with the lettering to do. How? It was at this stage I realised that I did have some creative ability, and I was thrilled to find that I could produce a reasonably acceptable set of letters.

Our first banner was complete, but what could we do with it? Two days later we proudly showed it off to friends, who immediately asked if they could use it the next evening. At a Youth Fellowship meeting they would be singing a chorus about peace, with dancing; the banner would emphasise the theme. The Lord obviously knew all about that banner and its use long before we did.

Our banner group was established and we had learnt two important lessons which apply not only to banner making, but the Christian life as well. We had learnt that God can tell us very specifically what to do, without showing us the reason until we have completed the task. We had also learnt that God takes what we give Him, and makes our gift into what He wants it to be.

At present we are a group of five very different people. We all have different natures, different styles of clothing, different ways of furnishing our houses, different talents and abilities, and between us we have an enormous variety of scrap materials. Also there are a large number of texts from the Bible that can be used for each banner.

We always end up in absolute agreement about the text, colour, design and materials. We do not get chaos. Despite indecisions, uncertainties, struggles there is one thing that brings all together, that unites each member of the group, that gives us a purpose. It is our belief in Jesus and in His power to guide us and show us the way with our banners just as he does with our lives. This is illustrated by a banner we made for a women's meeting, entitled 'The Christian Family'. The verse the Lord gave us for this banner, which shows a family standing with their arms raised in praise, was 'Seek ye first the Kingdom of God'. Whether this is in our family life, in our banner-making, in our church or community life, the secret is to 'Seek first the Kingdom of God', for only then will all the necessities of life be given to us.

There was an occasion when we learnt that our banner making was a special ministry that the Lord had given to us. We had been asked by a group of people from a nearby theological college, to make a banner depicting the text 'If it dies, it bears much fruit'. They explained a vision they had had of a seed that was beginning to shoot. We struggled and struggled with this one, we even changed the text, but of course that was not right. We looked at a banner made by another group on the same text (brown background with an ear of corn in off-white). That seemed to get us into an even bigger muddle. Eventually, after praying yet again, we began to realise just what making banners is all about. God had given to one group a vision of the seed as His direct word to them. He would use us to minister further to this group with a banner of a different design, a design that He wanted us to

use in this situation. Our position was to do what He said, not to copy what anyone else said, or even copy what He said to someone else. He would speak to us directly. After this things began to flow and we ended up with a brown seed exploding into a mass of orange and yellow petals. The lettering was in two colours, brown for the first part, 'If it dies,' and green to signify the growth of, 'it bears much fruit'.

What do banners mean to those involved? Above all, there is the excitement of producing something through which the Lord will speak, reassure, comfort and encourage His people.

The results are wider then we can see and we know that anything done for Him and with Him is infinitely worthwhile and satisfying. Then there is the joy given to those who receive. We sent small banners to two friends, both missionaries in Nepal, both showed verses the Lord gave us specially for them. In a letter from Susan, she said, 'Ina's banner is beautiful. Mine is hanging up on my wall. I'm sure it was a word from the Lord to me through you. Keep up the banner work.'

So you want to make a banner?

1. Choose a verse that is meaningful to you or is right for the church or setting where it will hang.

2. Find some background material suitable in colour and texture and cut it to the right size, allowing for turnings. Stitch hems and fold the top edge over to make a loop for the rod.

3. Decide on the style of lettering and sketch the words out together with the design, if required.

4. Cut the letters and design out in the desired materials and arrange on the background. Glue or pin, tack and stitch. Iron carefully.

5. Cut a dowel rod or other stick the required length. Buy cord and hang the banner.